APRIL 2016

Turkey in a Reconnecting Eurasia

Foreign Economic and Security Interests

AUTHOR
Ünal Çeviköz

EDITOR
Jeffrey Mankoff

Eurasia from the Outside In

A REPORT OF THE
CSIS RUSSIA AND EURASIA PROGRAM

CSIS | CENTER FOR STRATEGIC &
INTERNATIONAL STUDIES

ROWMAN &
LITTLEFIELD
Lanham • Boulder • New York • London

About CSIS

For over 50 years, the Center for Strategic and International Studies (CSIS) has worked to develop solutions to the world's greatest policy challenges. Today, CSIS scholars are providing strategic insights and bipartisan policy solutions to help decisionmakers chart a course toward a better world.

CSIS is a nonprofit organization headquartered in Washington, D.C. The Center's 220 full-time staff and large network of affiliated scholars conduct research and analysis and develop policy initiatives that look into the future and anticipate change.

Founded at the height of the Cold War by David M. Abshire and Admiral Arleigh Burke, CSIS was dedicated to finding ways to sustain American prominence and prosperity as a force for good in the world. Since 1962, CSIS has become one of the world's preeminent international institutions focused on defense and security; regional stability; and transnational challenges ranging from energy and climate to global health and economic integration.

Thomas J. Pritzker was named chairman of the CSIS Board of Trustees in November 2015. Former U.S. deputy secretary of defense John J. Hamre has served as the Center's president and chief executive officer since 2000.

CSIS does not take specific policy positions; accordingly, all views expressed herein should be understood to be solely those of the author(s).

ISBN: 978-1-4422-5930-0 (pb); 978-1-4422-5931-7 (eBook)

Center for Strategic & International Studies
1616 Rhode Island Avenue, NW
Washington, DC 20036
202-887-0200 | www.csis.org

Rowman & Littlefield
4501 Forbes Boulevard
Lanham, MD 20706
301-459-3366 | www.rowman.com

Contents

Preface

In January 2014, the CSIS Russia and Eurasia Program launched its Eurasia Initiative. The vast Eurasian landmass, stretching from China in the east to Europe in the west and from the Arctic Ocean in the north to the Indian Ocean in the south, includes some of the world's most powerful and dynamic states, as well as some of the world's most intractable challenges. Scholars and analysts are accustomed to focusing separately on Eurasia's various regions—Europe, the former Soviet Union, East Asia, South Asia, and Southeast Asia—rather than on the interactions between them. The goal of this initiative is to focus on these interactions, while analyzing and understanding Eurasia in a comprehensive way.

Today, more than any time since the collapse of the Silk Road five centuries ago, understanding these individual regions is impossible without also understanding the connections between them. Over the past two decades, Eurasia has begun to slowly reconnect, with the emergence of new trade relationships and transit infrastructures, as well as the integration of Russia, China, and India into the global economy. Even as this reconnection is under way, the center of economic dynamism in Eurasia, and in the world as a whole, continues shifting to the East. The impact of these shifts is potentially enormous, but they remain poorly understood because of intellectual and bureaucratic stovepiping in government and the broader analytic community.

Following its twin report series on Central Asia and on the South Caucasus, respectively, the CSIS Russia and Eurasia Program is now releasing papers in a third series we are informally calling "Eurasia from the Outside In." If the first two Eurasia Initiative report series focused on how economic connectivity and shifting political alignments looked from the interior of Eurasia, the current series focuses on the perspectives of the large, powerful countries that make up the periphery of the Eurasian landmass, namely China, India, Iran, Russia, and Turkey, as well as the European Union. The six reports in this series, each written by a leading local scholar of Eurasia, seek to provide insight into where Eurasia fits among the foreign economic and security priorities of these major powers.

While the most visible components of Eurasia's reconnection are infrastructure projects, the longer term result has been a reshuffling of relations between the post-Soviet states of Central

Asia and the South Caucasus on the one hand, and the major regional powers on the other. When the states of Central Asia and the South Caucasus became independent 25 years ago, they were closely tied to Russia. Over the past two and a half decades, they have developed a complex web of linkages to the other Eurasian powers, who themselves have devoted increased resources and attention to Eurasia in the years since the Soviet collapse. Russia still remains the dominant security provider in Central Asia and most of the South Caucasus. However China, the European Union, India, Iran, and Turkey all play major, if still evolving, roles in the region as well.

The scholars we have commissioned to write these reports bring a deep knowledge of their respective countries as well as a strong understanding of developments across Eurasia. While they are addressing a common set of questions, their answers and perspectives often diverge. Our goal is not consensus. Rather, it is to provide the best possible analysis of the roles these states are playing in shaping Eurasia's reconnection. We chose to seek out scholars from the countries being studied so that these reports would not be U.S.-centric, but would rather throw light on how Ankara, Beijing, Brussels, Moscow, New Delhi, and Tehran conceive of their respective interests and strategies in Eurasia.

With this report series, and indeed with the Eurasia Initiative more generally, we hope to encourage analysts and policymakers to think about Eurasia in a holistic way. Eurasia is much more than just the periphery of the old Soviet Union: it is a patchwork of states and peoples whose relationships are shifting rapidly. It is Central Asia, but it is also Europe; the South Caucasus but also India. Most importantly, it is the connections that are emerging and developing between these various states and regions. Our "Eurasia from the Inside Out" report series highlights the extent to which the comparatively small states at Eurasia's center have become a focal point for the economic and political engagement of the much larger powers surrounding them, and hence why these states continue to matter for global peace and prosperity.

Acknowledgments

Ambassador Çeviköz would like to acknowledge his appreciation to Ambassador Vural Altay, director general for Eastern Europe, Russia, Central Asia, and Caucasus; Mr. Gökhan Turan, deputy director general for Central Asia and Caucasus at the Ministry of Foreign Affairs of the Republic of Turkey in Ankara; as well as Mr. Yavuz Kül, consul general of Turkey in Nuremberg, for their invaluable support to gathering factual information on Eurasian politics. This report represents Ambassador Çeviköz's personal opinions and analysis on Turkey's role in Eurasia.

This report is made possible by the generous support of the Smith Richardson Foundation, the Carnegie Corporation of New York, the Ministry of Foreign Affairs of the Republic of Kazakhstan, and Carlos Bulgheroni. We are also extremely grateful for program support provided by the Carnegie Corporation of New York to the CSIS Russia and Eurasia Program.

The View from Ankara

In the last 25 years, Turkish foreign policy has gone through two significant readjustments. The first was mainly due to the collapse of the former Soviet Union in 1991, while the second stems from the rise, since 2002, of the Justice and Development Party (AKP) inside Turkey. The net result has been increased attention to the smaller states of Eurasia, with Ankara today focusing primarily on securing economic and trade benefits, including the promotion of new east–west transit infrastructure to Turkey. Despite the Turkic heritage of many Central Asian peoples, under the AKP Ankara has emphasized economic and energy interests more than ethnic solidarity, which has led it to focus mainly on the South Caucasus and Caspian Sea region, at the expense of the more remote, less resource-rich parts of Central Asia.

In the years immediately after the collapse of the Soviet Union, Turkey privileged linguistic and cultural affiliations in its relations with the new states of Eurasia. Azerbaijan, Turkmenistan, Uzbekistan, Kazakhstan, and Kyrgyzstan formed the extension of a "Turkic world" through the Caucasus into Central Asia. Although it was a joyful development for Turks to embrace their "brethren" in the new environment, the end of the Cold War, together with the disintegration of the USSR and the Warsaw Pact, also reduced the value of Turkey's strategic location to its partners in the North Atlantic Treaty Organization (NATO). This shifting perception led to an overall eastward reorientation of Turkish foreign policy.

Ankara aimed to become the main facilitator of the newly independent Turkic states' integration with the world political and economic system. Turkey's efforts focused on preparing the states for membership in the United Nations and the Organization for Security and Co-operation in Europe (OSCE) and enhancing their partnership relations with NATO through the North Atlantic Cooperation Council (NACC). This undertaking was not easy for Turkey, due to limited economic and financial resources. Despite such limitations, however, this period was characterized by some important initiatives, including the establishment of the Black Sea Economic Cooperation (BSEC) initiative, the formation of the Turkish International Cooperation and Development Agency (TİKA) to design development projects in the post-Soviet states, and the launching of the summit meetings of heads of states and governments among the six Turkic-speaking countries—namely, Turkey, Azerbaijan, Turkmenistan, Uzbekistan, Kyrgyzstan, and Kazakhstan.

The second revision of Turkey's approach to Eurasia developed in response to the rise to power of the AKP following its victory in the November 2002 parliamentary elections. The AKP's emergence came shortly after the terrorist attacks of September 11, 2001 in the United States and the subsequent U.S. intervention into Afghanistan, events that together facilitated the development of a new approach to foreign policy in Ankara. Perceiving the changes in the international environment as sources of both risks and opportunities, Turkey under the AKP embarked on a new foreign policy inspired by then professor Ahmet Davutoğlu's theoretical framework, depicted in his book *Strategic Depth*.[1]

Davutoğlu believed that the end of Cold War offered a historic opportunity for Turkey to become a global power, one that required an expansionist foreign policy based on Islamist ideology.[2] This expansive foreign policy vision would, according to Davutoğlu, allow Turkey to dominate its hinterland—the Middle East, the Balkans, and the Caucasus—and create a new sphere of influence. Davutoğlu's vision was underpinned more by power than by ethics, and he frequently made reference to concepts long abandoned in the West such as "Lebensraum."[3] As an adviser to then prime minister Recep Tayyip Erdoğan, Davutoğlu was unable to put his pan-Islamist policies into action because, then foreign minister Abdullah Gül sought to pursue a more realistic and Western-oriented approach.[4] Davutoğlu's subsequent role as foreign minister (2009–2014) and then prime minister (2014–present) in successive AKP governments provided an opportunity to implement these ideas in practice.

Davutoğlu sees a continuity between the Caucasus and the east side of the Caspian Sea, which together comprise the gateway to Asia. Davutoğlu views these locales, together with their immediate neighbors (Russia, Turkey, and Iran), as comprising a unified region that extends through the Caspian basin to Uzbekistan, Kazakhstan, and Turkmenistan.[5]

The Turkish political elite and foreign policymakers have, however, increasingly internalized the critical differences between the Caucasus, on the one hand, and Central Asia, on the other, and

---

1. Ahmet Davutoğlu, *Stratejik Derinlik: Türkiye'nin Uluslararası Konumu* (Istanbul: Küre Yayınları, 2009).

2. Behlül Özkan, "Turkey, Davutoğlu, and the Idea of Pan-Islamism," *Survival: Global Politics and Strategy* 56, no. 4 (August–September 2014): 119–140. Here, "expansionism" is not used in the territorial sense but in terms of expanding a "sphere of influence." For further reference to interpretations on Davutoğlu's ideas, see Ümit Kıvanç, *Pan-İslamcının Macera Kılavuzu* (Istanbul: Birikim Yayınları, 2015).

3. "Early writings reveal the real Davutoğlu," *Al Monitor*, August 13, 2014, http://www.al-monitor.com/pulse/originals /2014/08/zaman-davutoglu-ideologue-behlul-ozkan-academic-akp-islamic.html#.

4. Ibid.

5. Davutoğlu, *Stratejik Derinlik*, 125. Davutoğlu actually defines the changing international positioning of the Caucasus in relation to three planes: (1) the change in global balance and its effect on the region, (2) the regional plane itself, and (3) intraregional balance and contradictions, which include ethnic and religious diversification. For him, competition between Russia, Turkey, and Iran in the regional plane contains both the ramifications of the global competition in the first plane and the geopolitical and diplomatic maneuverings of the regional actors in the second one. This second plane—namely, the regional plane—is important because the policies of its regional actors such as Russia, Turkey, and Iran have implications for the Black Sea and the Balkans as well as for the Middle East and Central Asia.

begun to develop more tailor-made policies, with bilateralism proving more sustainable than regionalism. At the same time, the AKP's foreign policy gave top priority to the Middle East.

During the early 1990s, the government of Turgut Özal tried to reach out to Eurasia without changing the fundamental principles of Turkey's alliance with the West, seeking to work together with the United States during and after the Gulf War. The AKP government, however, preferred to develop a broader anti-status-quo vision and tried to dissociate itself from U.S. policies, particularly but not exclusively in the Middle East, symbolized by the Turkish Parliament's March 1, 2003 vote against allowing U.S. troops to intervene in Iraq from Turkish territory. This new "non-first-world axis" and "anti-Özalian" vision has become the main basis for current Turkish foreign policy conduct.[6]

Both of these readjustments had repercussions for Turkey's policy in Eurasia. Turkey's engagement in Eurasia had three phases between 1989 and 1995.[7] From 1989–1991, Turkey avoided overt support for the emerging nationalist movements among the Turkic peoples of the Soviet Union, maintaining its links with the Caucasus and Central Asia primarily through Moscow. Between 1991 and 1993, Turkey tried to benefit from the emergence of a possible Turkic "hinterland" with which it could easily establish relations due to linguistic and traditional commonalities. Ankara believed that the newly independent states would also be inspired by Turkey's democratic, secular, and Western-oriented state system and be inclined to identify their development schemes more with the Turkish example rather than those of Iran or Russia. Many argue that Turkey's approach to Central Asia at that time started to acquire pan-Turkic, Turanian, and pan-Islamist colorings and that Turkey had embarked on a race to create a new sphere of influence, though without substantial planning or programs.[8]

In the third phase, between 1993 and 1995, Russia was becoming more effective at filling the gap that emerged in the post-Soviet space after the collapse of the USSR.[9] After 1995, Turkey accepted this reality in Central Asia and started to implement a more prudent foreign policy in the region, one premised on avoiding possible confrontation with Russia.[10]

Turkey's conduct in Eurasia under the AKP is mainly motivated by the disappointment the country encountered in Central Asia in the 1990s. Under AKP rule Turkey started to focus more on energy issues and therefore began to place more emphasis on the Caucasus and the Caspian region, rather than Central Asia as such.[11]

In the South Caucasus, Turkey has developed intensive relations with Azerbaijan and Georgia. Azerbaijan is one of Turkey's major energy suppliers through the Baku-Tbilisi-Ceyhan (BTC) oil

6. Henry J. Barkey, "Turkey and the Great Powers," in *Turkey's Engagement with Modernity: Conflict and Change in the Twentieth Century*, ed. Celia Kerslake, Kerem Öktem, and Philip Robins (London: Palgrave Macmillan, 2010), 254. In defining AKP's foreign policy, Barkey argues that the AKP government "has little attachment to NATO and the other institutions and remnants of the Cold War and, therefore, feels no particular closeness to the U.S."

7. Baskın Oran, ed., *Türk Dış Politikası Cilt 2* (Istanbul: İletişim Yayınları, 2005), 371.

8. Ibid., 372.

9. Ibid.

10. Ibid.

11. Baskın Oran, ed., *Türk Dış Politikası Cilt 3* (Istanbul: İletişim Yayınları, 2013), 466.

pipeline as well as the Baku-Tbilisi-Erzurum natural gas pipeline. These two regional pipelines, coupled with the newly developed Baku-Tbilisi-Kars (BTK) railroad project, bring the three countries closer and bind them through energy, communications, and transport links. Turkey's Caucasus policy, however, lacks integrity and comprehensiveness due to the absence of diplomatic relations with Armenia. The Turkish-Armenian border has remained closed since April 3, 1993, in response to Armenia's occupation of Azerbaijani territory in and surrounding Nagorno-Karabakh. The nonequidistant, discriminative policy exposes Turkey to vulnerabilities and prevents it from fulfilling the role of an honest broker in the South Caucasus.

In Central Asia, Turkey confronts a more cohesive geographical setting. The five countries of the region have varying levels of authoritarian regimes (perhaps with the exception of Kyrgyzstan), and their secular tradition does not allow radical political Islam to easily flourish. Turkey, with its apparent emphasis on energy issues, has developed closer relations with hydrocarbon-rich Turkmenistan and Kazakhstan. Relations with Uzbekistan are the weakest link for Turkey in Central Asia. Nevertheless, over time business, civil society organizations, and family relations have helped to develop a deeper social interdependence between all the countries of the region and Turkey.

Turkey's ambition to establish a commonwealth of Turkic-speaking countries together with Azerbaijan, Kazakhstan, Kyrgyzstan, Turkmenistan, and Uzbekistan has gone through a difficult process. The summit meetings of the heads of states and governments of these countries, in time, were reduced to an exercise among only four countries, with Uzbekistan and Turkmenistan dropping out. Turkmenistan, although participating in the meetings out of courtesy, justified its reserved approach in terms of its policy of "active neutrality." Uzbekistan, on the other hand, distanced itself from the outset out of concern for its sovereignty and mistrust of Turkey. As a result, the Cooperation Council of Turkic Speaking States, formally established in Nakhichevan on October 3, 2009, is composed solely of Turkey, Azerbaijan, Kyrgyzstan, and Kazakhstan.

Nearly 25 years after the collapse of the USSR, whether Turkey will become an influential regional actor in the Caucasus is very much dependent on the future of its relations with Armenia. In Central Asia, relations with Uzbekistan will remain the key to the success of wider regional integration schemes. Turkey's overall policy in Eurasia, therefore, will continue to center on developing bilateral relations with key partner states in these two geographies, as well as on a careful coordination of its policies with other stakeholders in the same theater. The policies of Russia in particular, as well as of Iran, China, India, and Pakistan, and the European Union and the United States will be important variables in shaping Turkey's foreign policy in Eurasia.

Turkey's Foreign Economic and Security Policy in Eurasia

Turkey's geostrategic position at the crossroads of Europe and Eurasia allows it to play a unique role in the wider region. On the one hand, Turkey is an integral part of Europe. Its membership in European and Euro-Atlantic institutions keeps Turkey firmly anchored in the West. Already a member of NATO, the Council of Europe, the OSCE, and the Organization for Economic Co-operation and Development (OECD), Turkey aspires to become a member of the European Union as well.[1] EU membership still remains a strategic objective of Turkish foreign policy, despite repeated delays.[2]

On the other hand, Turkey plays a pivotal role in Eurasia as well, with its location astride the Balkans, the Black Sea, the Caucasus and Central Asia, the Middle East, the Eastern Mediterranean, and North Africa. Therefore, Turkey's foreign economic and security policy emphasizes the quest for synergy between its Western vocation and its immediate neighborhood. This geographic position encourages both a constant exploitation of opportunities for improvement and a diversification of Turkey's foreign economic relations.

To promote friendship and economic cooperation with all countries within these parameters, Turkey is impelled to attach primary importance to relations with Europe at large. No matter how Turkey's economic and commercial relations have diversified in the last decade, the European Union remains its main economic and foreign trade partner. Moreover, the know-how and technology needed to sustain Turkey's economic development still comes primarily from Europe. Turkey is a young, dynamic, and growing economy offering vast opportunities for foreign investment, as well as a large market for high-quality European consumption goods.

At the same time, the security and economic problems in Turkey's immediate neighborhood are worsening. For the foreseeable future, the most significant threats to Turkey's security will

---

1. Turkey's associate membership in the European Union dates back to the 1963 Ankara Agreement. Turkey applied for full membership in the European Union on April 14, 1987 and the Customs Union between Turkey and the European Union entered into force on January 1, 1996. The decision to start the accession negotiations was taken on December 17, 2004, and the talks started on October 3, 2005.

2. Ahmet Davutoğlu, "Turkish Foreign Policy and the EU in 2010," *Turkish Policy Quarterly* 8, no. 3 (2009): 11–17.

continue to stem from the ongoing problems in the Middle East, particularly the war in Syria and the resulting refugee crisis. Turkey will in the years to come feel more vulnerable in its border provinces and is likely to be more focused on the problems of the Middle East and Eastern Mediterranean, with fewer resources available for an expansive policy toward Eurasia.

Meanwhile, Russia will preserve its status as one of the key actors in Central Asia and the Middle East, while Iran's deal with the five permanent members of the UN Security Council plus Germany (the P5+1) on its nuclear program will also open new horizons for Tehran. Efforts at creating new spheres of influence within Eurasia, therefore, will become increasingly competitive.

REGIONAL COOPERATION

With the disintegration of the USSR, Turkey engaged proactively with Eurasia to expand opportunities for its companies. It launched the Black Sea Economic Cooperation (BSEC) initiative in 1992 with a view to converting existing bilateral ties among the Black Sea littoral states into a multilateral scheme. Although BSEC does not envisage mechanisms for solving political problems and primarily focuses on business and economic cooperation, the fact that Azerbaijan and Armenia, Russia and Georgia, and Russia and Ukraine have sat and worked together around the same table for the realization of a common goal has to be seen as a constructive confidence-building measure. BSEC not only facilitates rapprochement between the countries of the region, but also benefits from the synergy created with the European Union, since BSEC partners Bulgaria, Greece, and Romania are also members of the European Union.

Turkey is also a member of the Economic Cooperation Organization (ECO). A Cold War project initiated by Turkey, Iran, and Pakistan in 1985, the ECO has been rejuvenated in recent years by Turkey's invitation to the Central Asian republics, Azerbaijan and Afghanistan, to become members, in the process creating an organization encompassing more than 300 million people and promoting economic, technical, and cultural cooperation among member states. The organization has embarked on several projects in priority sectors including energy, trade, transportation, agriculture, and drug control.

THE SOUTH CAUCASUS

Turkey has always perceived the Caucasus primarily through a strategic lens. On the one hand, the three South Caucasus countries on Turkey's eastern border represent a corridor for north–south as well as east–west transport and communications. After the collapse of the USSR, Turkey ceased having a direct land border with Russia. Accessing the Russian North Caucasus, homeland for millions of immigrants to Turkey in the late nineteenth century, now required transit across the independent states of the South Caucasus.

The South Caucasus is Turkey's gateway to Central Asia, too. Current transport and communication lines between Turkey and Azerbaijan through Georgia present uninterrupted physical continuity, particularly through the railroad system. The BTK railroad project, which is planned to start operations before the end of 2016, will facilitate a direct connection all the way from London to Beijing.

The South Caucasus is also important for Turkey because of energy. Rich in hydrocarbon resources, the Caspian basin makes the South Caucasus a prominent source of supply through the BTC crude oil pipeline, Baku-Tbilisi-Erzurum natural gas pipeline, and the planned Trans-Anatolian Natural Gas Pipeline (TANAP). These connections could be extended across the Caspian Sea to Turkmenistan, which would make the South Caucasus an even more important gateway for energy corridors between the east and the west. Turkey, through cooperation with Azerbaijan, expects to become a critical hub in those corridors, offering diversification of routes and supplies to Europe to enhance the EU's energy security policies.

It is necessary to caution, however, that in spite of all these positive factors in transport, communications, and energy, which suggest a rather optimistic vision for the future development and stability of the Caucasus region, there are a number of issues that can put these multilateral cooperation schemes at risk.

First of all, three protracted post–Cold War conflicts—namely, the problem of Nagorno-Karabakh between Azerbaijan and Armenia, as well as the problems between Georgia and Russia over Abkhazia and South Ossetia—limit opportunities for regional cooperation. The South Caucasus also faces systemic problems such as ethnic and religious tensions, territorial disputes, lack of trust and confidence, as well as transborder challenges such as migration, smuggling, illicit trafficking, and terrorism, which collectively constrain multilateral cooperation and prevent the countries of the region from overcoming their bilateral disputes.

Second, through the transport lines between the east and the west, the South Caucasus also presents an excellent opportunity for illicit trafficking and transborder organized crime.

Third, the region also suffers from an abundance of economic and social challenges connected to poverty, injustice, corruption, and unemployment, as well as widespread violations of human rights and democratic freedoms. These issues not only put the prospects for a more peaceful and stable South Caucasus at risk, but also present serious challenges to the stability and security of Turkey itself.

Turkey has always pursued a principled and uniform policy of supporting the territorial integrity and political unity of Azerbaijan and Georgia, in compliance with international law. Turkey, therefore, does not recognize the independence of Nagorno-Karabakh, Abkhazia, or South Ossetia. In line with the UN Charter, Turkey is also against the use or the threat of use of force to resolve these conflicts and supports the peaceful resolution of all the protracted conflicts in the region. This approach is at odds with Russia's recognition of the independence of Abkhazia and South Ossetia. In addition to its own nonrecognition policy, Turkey also supports the European Union's nonrecognition and engagement policy toward Abkhazia. Many Turkish citizens have relatives in Abkhazia who maintain trade and commerce with the large Abkhaz diaspora in Turkey (apart from Russia itself, Turkey is the largest trade partner for Abkhazia). Such economic ties are a source of concern for Georgia.[3]

---

3. Sergi Kapanadze, "Turkish Trade with Abkhazia: An Apple of Discord for Georgia," *Turkish Policy Quarterly* 13, no. 3 (Fall 2014): 59.

In light of these challenges, Turkey has opted for an approach to the region that emphasizes soft power. In Georgia and Azerbaijan, Turkey promotes its role as a trade and investment partner and looks for opportunities for expanding commercial relations through cooperation on infrastructure projects linking the three countries. This approach is vulnerable to disruption by instability in the region, forcing Turkey to become more engaged in addressing political problems in the South Caucasus in order to safeguard both its economic interests and the future of the trilateral cooperation it enjoys with Georgia and Azerbaijan.

Turkey's policy vis-à-vis the South Caucasus region is therefore based on the following principles:

- Development of regional stability and security,

- Facilitation of peaceful, lasting, and just solutions to the conflicts of the region,

- Support for the independence, sovereignty, and territorial integrity of the countries of the region,

- Ensuring the sustainability of democratization as well as economic and political reform processes in the region,

- Deepening of regional and inter-regional cooperation as well as bilateral and regional economic integration,

- Strengthening of the concept of regional ownership,

- Support for the development of relations between the countries of the region and Euro-Atlantic institutions.[4]

Turkey is a member of the Minsk Group established by the OSCE to address the Nagorno-Karabakh conflict. In 2008, after the Georgia-Russia war, Turkey also came forward with a proposal for multilateral cooperation in the South Caucasus, the so-called Caucasus Stability and Cooperation Platform (CSCP), which aimed at enhancing understanding and confidence among the countries of the region.[5] The CSCP brought together Turkey, Russia, Georgia, Azerbaijan, and Armenia for three successive meetings at the level of deputy foreign ministers. Although the CSCP did not become a concrete forum for cooperation, Ankara believes it still offers a good platform for promoting regional stability once existing conflicts are resolved.

Turkey's foreign policy in the Caucasus relies on both bilateral relations as well as trilateral cooperation schemes involving Azerbaijan and, in various combinations, Georgia, Iran, and Turkmenistan. Turkey has established a series of trilateral meetings among the foreign ministers of Turkey-Azerbaijan-Georgia, Turkey-Azerbaijan-Iran, and Turkey-Azerbaijan-Turkmenistan. Apart from the Azerbaijan-Iran-Turkey trilateral, these meetings also take place at the level of the heads of state.

Having first met on the sidelines of the ECO meeting in Istanbul in December 2010, the foreign ministers of Turkey, Iran, and Azerbaijan had their first formal meeting in Urumia, Iran, in April 2011.

---

4. For a general reference to Turkey's relations with the Caucasus countries, see the Republic of Turkey, Ministry of Foreign Affairs, "Turkey's Relations with Southern Caucasus Countries," last modified 2011, http://www.mfa.gov.tr /turkiye_nin-guney-kafkasya-ulkeleriyle-iliskileri.tr.mfa.

5. Ali Babacan, "Calming the Caucasus," *New York Times*, September 23, 2008.

Turkey, in a way, tried to thaw Azerbaijani-Iranian relations at a time when political tensions between Baku and Tehran remained high.[6] This trilateral scheme still continues; its most recent meeting took place in Van, Turkey, in March 2014.

The second trilateral scheme Turkey developed was between Turkey, Azerbaijan, and Turkmenistan, again at the level of foreign ministers, with the initial meeting held in Baku on May 26, 2014. The aim of this gathering is to enhance cooperation across various fields, such as energy, trade, transport, culture, tourism, education, and environmental protection[7] and is intended to be upgraded to the level of presidents in the future.

However, the most significant and sustainable trilateral scheme involves Turkey, Georgia, and Azerbaijan. Upon the invitation of Turkey, the foreign ministers of these three countries launched a series of meetings in 2012, which subsequently developed into a more comprehensive trilateral cooperation process. The first meeting took place in Trabzon, Turkey, on June 8, 2012, marking the 20th anniversary of the establishment of diplomatic relations. The declaration of this meeting announced the parties' "determination to build a better future for the region characterized by peace, stability, cooperation, and increasing wealth and welfare."[8] This trilateral cooperation process focuses on defense cooperation, harmonization of foreign-security policy, energy and transport cooperation, as well as business, trade, and commerce.

AZERBAIJAN

Azerbaijan is the main pillar of Turkey's policy toward the South Caucasus. Political relations have been upgraded to the level of strategic partnership with the formation of the High Level Strategic Cooperation Council (HLSCC) between the two countries in 2010.[9] The Council, through annual meetings, reviews the state of bilateral relations in political, economic, commercial, financial, energy, culture, customs, and security areas and advances new proposals for enhancing them.[10]

Nagorno-Karabakh underpins the solidarity between Turkey and Azerbaijan, but is also a source of tension. As a reaction to Armenia's occupation of seven Azerbaijani districts (Agdam, Fuzuli,

---

6. Fulya Özerkan, "Turkey seeks thaw in Iran-Azeri ties," *Hürriyet Daily News*, December 4, 2011.

7. Republic of Turkey, Ministry of Foreign Affairs, *Baku Statement of the First Trilateral Meeting of the Ministers of Foreign Affairs of the Republic of Azerbaijan, the Republic of Turkey and Turkmenistan, 26 May 2014, Baku*, http://www.mfa.gov.tr/baku-statement-of-the-first-trilateral-meeting-of-the-ministers-of-foreign-affairs-of-the-republic-of-azerbaijan_-the-republic.en.mfa.

8. Republic of Turkey, Ministry of Foreign Affairs, *Trabzon Declaration of the Ministers of Foreign Affairs of the Republic of Azerbaijan, Georgia and the Republic of Turkey, 08 June 2012, Trabzon*, http://www.mfa.gov.tr/trabzon—declaration-of-the-ministers-of-foreign-affairs-of-the-republic-of-azerbaijan_-georgia-and-the-republic-of-turkey_-08-june-2012_-trabzon.en.mfa.

9. *Hürriyet*, September 10, 2010.

10. The first High Level Strategic Cooperation Council (HLSCC) was formed between Turkey and Brazil with an agreement signed on January 19, 2006. Today Turkey has such councils with 14 countries—namely, Iraq, Syria, Russia, Greece, Azerbaijan, Lebanon, Pakistan, Ukraine, Kyrgyzstan, Egypt, Bulgaria, Kazakhstan, and Tunisia. See Republic of Turkey, Prime Ministry, Office of Public Diplomacy, *Yüksek Düzeyli İşbirliği Mekanizmaları*, last modified January 22, 2016, http://kdk.gov.tr/haber/yuksek-duzeyli-isbirligi-mekanizmalari/452.

Zangelan, Kelbajar, Jebrail, Kubatli, Lachin) surrounding Nagorno-Karabakh, Turkey has kept its border with Armenia closed since 1993 out of solidarity with Baku, while Ankara is the most ardent supporter of Azerbaijan's interests in international forums on Nagorno-Karabakh. From the Turkish perspective, the occupation of Azerbaijani territory by Armenia represents a gross violation of international law, as well as the principles of good-neighborly relations, respect for territorial integrity, and the peaceful resolution of conflicts. Turkey considers the problem of Nagorno-Karabakh one of the main obstacles to peace, security, and stability in the South Caucasus, as well as to multilateral cooperation throughout the region. As a member of the Minsk Group, Turkey at the same time tries to contribute to the resolution of this conflict and is also kept duly informed by the Group's cochairs (namely, the United States, Russia, and France) about the negotiations process.

Nagorno-Karabakh, however, has also resulted in setbacks to Turkish-Azerbaijani relations. The two protocols signed in Zürich on October 10, 2009, which crowned a two-year effort to normalize Turkish-Armenian relations, were not ratified in the Turkish Parliament because then prime minister Erdoğan made resolution of the Nagorno-Karabakh problem a precondition for the implementation of the protocols in response to both domestic pressure and intense lobbying from Baku.

Relations between Turkey and Azerbaijan have always encompassed military cooperation and security issues as well as political, social, economic, and commercial aspects. Relations were upgraded to a strategic partnership with the "Declaration on Deepened Strategic Cooperation" signed in May 1997. This declaration, in addition to providing for the transport of Azerbaijani oil via Turkey to international markets, also included a formal condemnation of Armenia's occupation of Nagorno-Karabakh and asked for withdrawal from the occupied territories. The negative effects of the 2009 attempt to normalize Turkish-Armenian relations led Ankara to offer further and stronger military cooperation to Baku, which was eventually secured with the signing of the "Agreement on Strategic Partnership and Mutual Assistance" during the visit of Turkish president Abdullah Gül to Baku on August 16–17, 2010.[11]

With its large economy and heavy energy demand, Turkey has also become an increasingly attractive market for Azerbaijan's energy sector. In 2014, bilateral trade was $5.1 billion with Turkey enjoying a surplus of $0.65 billion. Turkey's trade volume with Azerbaijan increased by 200 percent between 2006 and 2014. The primary Turkish exports to Azerbaijan are iron and steel, furniture, and precious metals. Turkish imports from Azerbaijan are mainly natural gas, crude oil, and raw aluminum. Turkey's investments in Azerbaijan amount to $9 billion, of which $4.8 billion is the Turkish Petroleum Agency's investments in Azerbaijan's energy sector. Turkey is also believed to be one of the main sources of foreign investment in the Azerbaijani economy in nonenergy sectors. Around 2,600 Turkish companies operate in Azerbaijan. Azerbaijan is also one of the largest sources of inward investment to Turkey, with foreign direct investment (FDI) valued at up to $4 billion,

---

11. "Agreement on Strategic Partnership and Mutual Assistance between the Republic of Turkey and the Republic of Azerbaijan" was signed in Baku on August 16, 2010 and ratified on April 26, 2011. See Resmi Gazete [Official Gazette], May 28, 2011. This agreement entails military cooperation between the two countries in case of a military attack or aggression against either of the countries.

Table 2.1. Trade between Turkey and Azerbaijan

Years	Exports	Imports	Volume	Balance
2010	1,550	865	2,415	685
2011	2,063	1,388	3,453	677
2012	2,584	1,638	4,222	946
2013	2,960	1,726	4,686	1,233
2014	2,876	2,229	5,105	646
2013–2014 %	−2.8%	29.1%	8.9%	−47.6%

Source: Turkish Statistical Institute, Ministry of Economy (in million U.S. dollars).

mainly in energy. For instance, the State Oil Company of Azerbaijan (SOCAR) started to operate in the Turkish market in 2008, purchasing 51 percent of the shares in Turcas Petrol. With a further purchase of 25 percent of the company in 2011, SOCAR established a joint venture worth $2.6 billion.[12] With its further goal of integrating petro-chemistry, energy, and logistics on the Petkim Peninsula, as well as the TANAP project, SOCAR's total investments in Turkey are expected to surpass $20 billion by 2018.[13]

ARMENIA

Turkish-Armenian relations represent the weakest link in Turkey's South Caucasus policy. Although Turkey recognized the independence of Armenia in 1991, the two countries never established diplomatic relations. The most intensive efforts to normalize relations occurred during 2008–2009. This process, facilitated by Switzerland and enhanced by the famous "football diplomacy"— reciprocal visits of the presidents of the two countries to watch the European Championship quali- fication games between Turkey and Armenia—culminated in the signing of the two Zürich protocols that would, respectively, normalize relations and end Turkey's support to Azerbaijan's policy of blockading Armenia. Although these protocols would be the most significant step forward between the two countries since the 1921 Treaty of Kars,[14] they never came forward for ratification in the Turkish Parliament because of disputes over their connection to the Nagorno-Karabakh problem.

12. "Petkim Azerilerin oldu," *Sabah*, December 31, 2011, http://www.sabah.com.tr/ekonomi/2011/12/31/petkim -azerilerin-oldu.

13. "Socar'dan Star Rafineri için Dev imza," *Akşam*, June 6, 2014.

14. Treaty of Kars was signed in the Turkish east Anatolian city of Kars on October 13, 1921, between the Government of the Turkish Grand National Assembly and the three Soviet Republics in the Caucasus (Armenia, Azerbaijan, and Georgia) and is still in effect. Basically, it defines the current boundaries between Turkey and Georgia, Turkey and Armenia, and the status of Nakhichevan as an autonomous territory under the protection of Azerbaijan.

Armenia also suspended the ratification process in its own parliament, mainly due to the pressure exerted on the country's leadership by the Armenian diaspora, with Armenian president Serzh Sargsyan finally withdrawing the two protocols from the Armenian Parliament in February 2015.

Another significant dispute between Armenia and Turkey is the question of how to define and recognize the events of 1915, which the Armenian side considers to be an act of genocide while Turkey, although acknowledging mutual massacres between Turks and the Armenians during the First World War, refuses to label the events of 1915 as genocide on the basis on the 1948 UN Convention on Genocide.

Despite the absence of diplomatic relations and the closed land border between the two countries, there is limited trade between Turkey and Armenia. The volume of trade is believed to be around $234 million, of which 99 percent is Turkish exports to Armenia, mainly consumer goods and food. Still, this figure accounts for just 5.6 percent of overall Armenian imports.[15] With the border closed, Turkish consumer goods reach Armenia mainly through Georgia. Thrice weekly flights between Yerevan and Istanbul by Turkey's Atlas Air also allow many Armenian citizens to come to Turkey and find temporary jobs in the Turkish labor market.

GEORGIA

Bilateral relations with Turkey developed rapidly following Georgia's independence from the Soviet Union. Georgia sits astride the main transit route between Turkey and Russia on the one hand and Turkey, Azerbaijan, and Central Asia on the other, while Turkey is Georgia's main outlet to the west.

Georgia's geographical location has allowed it to become a major partner for both Turkey and Azerbaijan in the development of trilateral projects, mainly in energy and transport. The oil and gas pipelines between Azerbaijan and Turkey via Georgia, as well as the Baku-Tbilisi-Kars railroad project, are the most concrete examples of this trilateral cooperation. The partnership has allowed the three countries to organize a trilateral forum at the level of foreign ministers, defense ministers, ministers of economy, ministers of transport, chiefs of the general staff, chairmen of parliaments' foreign policy commissions, as well as business forums. The trilateral meetings have recently been upgraded to the level of presidents as well. As a result of these intensive relations, Turkey has proposed establishing a High Level Strategic Cooperation Council with Georgia.

Turkey supports Georgia's efforts at integration with Euro-Atlantic structures and defends its territorial integrity. Turkey does not recognize the independence of Abkhazia and South Ossetia, in spite of the presence of a considerable Abkhaz diaspora, estimated at around 120,000, in Turkey.[16] Defense and military cooperation between the two countries, however, remains limited to Turkey's

---

15. There are no Turkish records on Turkish-Armenian trade relations because there is no direct trade between the two countries. The figures mentioned here refer to Armenian sources.

16. The number of Turkish citizens with their ethnic origins from the Caucasus is not clear. Different sources give the number as between 2 million and 8 million. Generally they are known to be composed of Abkhaz, Adigey, Avar, Nogay, and Malkars, but overall they are categorized as Circassians. Today, the number of Abkhaz living in Abkhazia is cited to be around 120,000. The number of Abkhaz living in Turkey is believed to be more than the total number of Abkhaz living in Abkhazia proper.

Table 2.2. Trade between Turkey and Georgia

Years	Exports	Imports	Volume	Balance
2010	770	291	1,060	479
2011	1,092	314	1,406	778
2012	1,254	180	1,434	1,073
2013	1,246	201	1,448	1,045
2014	1,444	232	1,676	1,212
2013–2014 %	16%	15%	16%	16%

Source: Turkish Statistical Institute, Ministry of Economy (in million U.S. dollars).

assistance in modernizing Georgia's technological capacity to bring it closer to NATO standards. Turkey has also been quite vocal in its support for Georgia's NATO membership aspirations.

Since 2007, Turkey has been Georgia's biggest trade partner. Turkey is also one of the main sources of Georgian FDI. Since the end of 2011, Turkish and Georgian citizens can travel reciprocally without passports (needing only national IDs). This development has allowed numerous Georgian citizens to find seasonal or even permanent jobs in Turkey. The volume of trade between the two countries is around $1.6 billion—85 percent of which is Turkish exports to Georgia. Turkey exports plastic products, iron and steel, and machinery to Georgia and imports scrap metal, textiles, and agricultural goods.

CENTRAL ASIA

Despite a shared Turkic identity, Turkey's role in Central Asia remains underdeveloped. In the early 1990s, Turkish officials rejoiced at gaining access to their fellow Turks and sought to build on the historical, cultural, linguistic, and traditional affiliations with the peoples of Central Asia. In practice, most of the initial contacts were at the highest political level, as the strongly presidential systems prevailing in Central Asia did not allow development of more institutionalized relations with Ankara at the intergovernmental level or between representatives of the business and civil society sectors. The frequency of such high-level contacts, therefore, depended mainly on the willingness of Turkish presidents Turgut Özal and Süleyman Demirel and foreign minister Hikmet Çetin to prioritize relations with their Central Asian counterparts.[17]

In addition, in the 1990s, some of the Central Asian states accused Turkey of supporting dissident movements, due primarily to the involvement of some Turkish citizens in coup attempts against

---

17. Oran, *Türk Dış Politikası Cilt 3*, 470.

the presidents of Azerbaijan, Turkmenistan, and Uzbekistan. In Azerbaijan, police special forces (OMON) under the control of the former prime minister Suret Hüseynov plotted a coup attempt against President Heydar Aliyev on March 13, 1995. Turkish president Süleyman Demirel informed Aliyev about the attempt at the last moment, preventing the coup from taking place. Two Turkish citizens working for TİKA were arrested.[18] Similarly, Uzbekistan accused the perpetrators of a February 1999 bomb attack targeting President Islam Karimov of having links to Turkish citizens, due to contacts between Tahir Yoldashev, the leader of Islamic Movement of Uzbekistan, and former Turkish prime minister Necmettin Erbakan.[19] In Turkmenistan, a coup attempt against President Saparmurat Niyazov on November 25, 2002 resulted in the arrest of six Turkish citizens believed to be among the perpetrators.[20] The real or suspected involvement of Turkish citizens, some with connections to leading political circles in Ankara, in these coup attempts contributed to the fading away of Turkey's already-weak influence in the region.

The AKP's rise to power in November 2002 was seen in Central Asia as consolidating the Islamist policies mostly identified with Erbakan and created serious concern in Central Asian countries. Elites in these countries had internalized secularism, if not atheism, during 70 years of Soviet rule and perceived of the new AKP government as a threat to the secularist political model prevailing in the region.

The launch of the Shanghai Cooperation Organization (SCO) in 2002 and the U.S.-led military intervention in Afghanistan also contributed to the sidelining of Turkish influence, while Russia, China, and the United States became the major external actors in Central Asia.[21] Even as Turkish political influence waned, Turkey's relations with Central Asia started to develop in a more institutionalized manner through an expanding network of social, economic, and family relations, and thanks to the efforts of businessmen and Turkish citizens who settled in the region in the early 2000s.[22] For instance, Çalık Holding became a prominent investor in Turkmenistan's textile industry and power plant construction, while Sembol Construction Company and several Turkish investors became prominent construction contractors in Kazakhstan.

The Cooperation Council of Turkic Speaking States, which was established in Nakhichevan on October 3, 2009, provides the opportunity to promote multilateral cooperation among Turkey, Azerbaijan, Kazakhstan, and Kyrgyzstan. Turkey has also established HLSCC mechanisms with Kazakhstan and Kyrgyzstan and a Cooperation Council with Tajikistan.

In 2014, Turkey's trade turnover with Central Asia as a whole reached $9.5 billion. Turkey has played a leading role in the establishment of free-market rules as well as the development of small and medium-sized entreprises in the region. Turkish businessmen and investors are particularly active in the construction sector. Turkish construction companies have taken on over $73 billion worth of projects in Kazakhstan, Kyrgyzstan, Uzbekistan, and Turkmenistan. In Turkmenistan alone, the figure is $50 billion.

---

18. Ibid., 471.

19. Ibid.

20. Ibid.

21. Ibid., 470.

22. Ibid.

Table 2.3. Trade between Turkey and Kazakhstan

Years	Exports	Imports	Volume	Balance
2010	818.9	2471.0	3289.9	−1652.1
2011	947.8	3020.0	3967.8	−2072.2
2012	1068.6	3371.0	4439.6	−2302.4
2013	1039.4	3106.1	4145.5	−2066.8
2014	977.8	2453.4	3431.3	−1475.6
2013–2014 %	−6%	−21%	−17%	−29%

Source: Turkish Statistical Institute, Ministry of Economy (in million U.S. dollars).

KAZAKHSTAN

Turkey's relations with Kazakhstan have developed steadily. As an energy-rich country, Kazakhstan plays an important role in Turkey's economic and commercial links with Central Asia. Kazakhstan is also connected across the Caspian Sea to the BTC oil pipeline, which allows it to export oil to European markets and Turkey. In the first ten months of 2014, Kazakhstan exported 10.15 million barrels of crude oil through the BTC. Although Kazakhstan committed to provide around 14.66 million barrels a year, Astana planned to pump only 6.6 million barrels into the BTC in 2015, a shortfall Kazakh authorities have explained as resulting from "technical difficulties."

The two countries also established an HLSCC in 2012.[23] Around 100 Turkish businessmen have invested some $2 billion in Kazakhstan in the food, petroleum, pharmaceuticals and chemicals, construction, hotels, health, and defense industries. Trade relations have also been developing steadily. Turkey mainly exports jewelery articles, plastic goods, construction materials, and carpets to Kazakhstan and imports crude oil, natural gas, raw and refined copper, raw zinc and aluminum, raw lead, and wheat.

UZBEKISTAN

Turkey's political, economic, and commercial relations with Uzbekistan fall short of their potential. Uzbek president Islam Karimov does not see Turkey as a reliable partner, mainly because of contacts between Turkey and Uzbek dissident movements. Prominent Uzbek dissident Mohammad Salih's contacts in Turkey remain a serious obstacle to better bilateral relations; Salih is

---

23. Doğan Yıldız, "Kazakistan'la Türkiye arasında stratejik işbirliği konseyi kuruldu," *Cihan Haber Ajansı*, May 23, 2012, https://www.cihan.com.tr/tr/kazakistanla-turkiye-arasinda-stratejik-isbirligi-konseyi-kuruldu-709292.htm.

Table 2.4. Trade between Turkey and Uzbekistan

Years	Exports	Imports	Volume	Balance
2010	282.7	861.4	1144.0	−578.7
2011	354.5	939.9	1294.4	−585.4
2012	449.9	813.3	1263.2	−363.4
2013	562.5	815.4	1377.9	−252.9
2014	603.4	780.7	1384.1	−177.3
2013−2014 %	7%	−4%	−0.4%	−30%

Source: Turkish Statistical Institute, Ministry of Economy (in million U.S. dollars).

also rumored to be married to a relative of Turkish president Erdoğan's wife. Karimov accuses Turkey of involvement in plots to overthrow his government, most notably the 1999 Tashkent bombing.

Since the beginning of 2014, a new process of rapprochement has started. Then prime minister Erdoğan and Uzbek president Karimov met in February 2014 in Sochi, Russia, followed by meetings between Foreign Minister Davutoğlu and his Uzbek counterpart, as well as with President Karimov when Davutoğlu visited Tashkent in July 2014. This visit was the first high-level visit from Turkey to Uzbekistan in 13 years. While these contacts contributed to a thaw in relations, a planned visit to Turkey by Uzbek foreign minister Abdulaziz Kamilov at the beginning of 2015 was abruptly canceled while a scheduled April 2015 meeting of the Joint Economic Commission, tasked to coordinate regularly the economic, commercial, and trade relations between the two countries, was also postponed.

Trade relations between the two countries are also underdeveloped due to tight monetary policies in Uzbekistan, delays in repatriation of profits, bureaucratic obstacles, the arbitrariness in commercial inspections, as well as difficulties with Uzbekistan's banking system. In spite of all these negative factors, Turkey is Uzbekistan's fifth largest trade partner. Turkish exports mainly focus on the textile industry, motor vehicles, and electrical appliances, while imports are generally refined copper, cotton thread, and petroleum products.

KYRGYZSTAN

A relatively small economy, Kyrgyzstan has always been looking for aid and assistance from Turkey. Turkey has extended $855 million worth of developmental aid to Kyrgyzstan in economic-commercial projects, health, education, and sociocultural cooperation programs. Turkey formed an HLSCC with Kyrgyzstan in 2011 to promote bilateral trade and has also been involved in the

Table 2.5. Trade between Turkey and Kyrgyzstan

Years	Exports	Imports	Volume	Balance
2010	129,202	30,900	160,102	98,302
2011	180,241	52,123	232,364	128,118
2012	257,470	45,226	302,697	212,244
2013	388,336	36,964	425,300	351,372
2014	421,980	65,648	487,628	356,332
2013–2014 %	9%	78%	15%	1%

Source: Turkish Statistical Institute, Ministry of Economy (in thousand U.S. dollars).

introduction of small and medium-sized enterprises into the Kyrgyz economy. Turkish investments in Kyrgyzstan have reached $1 billion.

Trade relations are relatively small due to the scale of Kyrgyz economy. Turkish exports are woven carpets, precious metals, and textile goods. Turkish imports are beans, cotton, copper, and gold.

Corruption and arbitrary inspections, along with high taxation, deter many Turkish businessmen from maintaining their businesses in the country. Turkey is concerned as well that Kyrgyzstan's membership in the Eurasian Economic Union may have further negative effects on Turkish-Kyrgyz bilateral trade relations.

TURKMENISTAN

Turkish-Turkmen relations developed quite steadily during the initial years after the Soviet collapse because Turkey offered Turkmenistan an opening to the west and an opportunity to transfer gas to European markets via the Caspian Sea and Azerbaijan. Turkey's preference for the Blue Stream project with Russia, rather than the development of projects involving Turkmen gas, however, soured bilateral relations in the 1990s. Relations were further negatively affected by the suspected participation of some Turkish citizens in the coup attempt against President Niyazov in 2002.

Erdoğan's visit to Turkmenistan in January 2003, shortly before he became prime minister, marked a turning point, with Erdoğan condemning the previous year's "terrorist attempt." Turkmenistan soon reversed its distant position toward Turkey and trade relations started to grow rapidly, increasing fivefold from 2003 to 2011. Turkish investments in Turkmenistan by the end of 2011 reached $30 billion. Today this figure has reached $50 billion, which puts Turkmenistan first among the Central Asian states in the value of Turkish investment. Most of this investment is in the nonenergy sector, particularly focusing on construction projects.

Table 2.6. Trade between Turkey and Turkmenistan

Years	Exports	Imports	Volume	Balance
2010	1139.8	386.3	1526.2	753.5
2011	1493.3	392.7	1886.0	1100.6
2012	1480.1	303.5	1783.6	1176.5
2013	1957.5	653.8	2611.3	1303.7
2014	2232.8	624.1	2856.9	1608.7
2013–2014 %	14%	−5%	9%	23%

Source: Turkish Statistical Institute, Ministry of Economy (in million U.S. dollars).

As a Caspian littoral state, Turkmenistan also has an important role to play in projects connecting the Caucasus to Central Asia. Turkey has always supported carrying Turkmen gas across the Caspian via the proposed Trans-Caspian Gas Pipeline (TCGP), in tandem with Azerbaijan. Disputes over the status of the Caspian among the five littoral states, along with differences between Ashgabat and Baku, however, have prevented progress toward building the pipeline.

Following the visit of Turkmen president Gurbanguly Berdimuhammedov to Ankara on March 4, 2015, Erdoğan announced a trilateral mechanism on energy cooperation between Turkey, Azerbaijan, and Turkmenistan. Pending a resolution of the status of the Caspian Sea, however, progress on Azerbaijani-Turkmen cooperation looks quite dim. Nevertheless, this new trilateral mechanism may facilitate more of an energy dialogue between Baku and Ashgabat in the future.[24]

Turkish-Turkmen trade relations have grown steadily but slowly. Turkey's exports to Turkmenistan are three times higher than imports, though Ankara has offered to sign a preferential trade agreement with Turkmenistan to balance trade relations. Turkish exports to Turkmenistan are mainly iron and steel, electrical conductors, and gold, while Turkey imports cotton and petroleum products from Turkmenistan.

Turkmenistan also has an important place in the transportation projects connecting the two sides of the Caspian Sea. Turkey has recently participated as the fifth party to the Afghanistan-Turkmenistan-Azerbaijan-Georgia quadrilateral format on transit transportation organized jointly by Turkmenistan and the European Union–backed Transport Corridor Europe-Caucasus-Asia (TRACECA) forum. This transport and transit corridor project intends to promote Afghanistan's socioeconomic revival and allow it to join major regional and international infrastructure projects. It also aims to increase the volume of general trade and reduce expenditures on cargo transit.

24. Zaur Shiriyev, "Turkmenistan, Turkey, and Azerbaijan: A Trilateral Energy Strategy?," *Eurasia Daily Monitor* 12, no. 45 (March 11, 2015), http://www.jamestown.org/programs/edm/single/?tx_ttnews%5Btt_news%5D=43646&cHash=86f66 6dcea499441a42e5276d2255b1f#.VtBxCvkrLcs.

Table 2.7. Trade between Turkey and Tajikistan

Years	Exports	Imports	Volume	Balance
2010	143,890	283,689	427,580	–139,799
2011	172,575	324,283	496,858	–151,707
2012	234,947	345,178	580,125	–110,231
2013	283,620	371,358	654,978	–87,738
2014	277,505	160,947	438,452	116,558
2013–2014 %	–2%	–57%	–33%	233%

Source: Turkish Statistical Institute, Ministry of Economy (in thousand U.S. dollars).

TAJIKISTAN

With a majority Persian-speaking population, Tajikistan has not been involved in Turkish-sponsored projects to promote cooperation among the Turkic peoples of the Caucasus and Central Asia. The two countries have nonetheless developed decent bilateral relations. Tajik leaders have been particularly interested in attracting Turkish business and investors, although Tajikistan has a very limited place in Turkey's trade with Central Asia. Although Turkey kept its embassy in Dushanbe open during the civil war between 1992 and 1997, economic and trade relations developed very slowly. The small size of the Tajik economy, as well as the limited transportation potential resulting from Tajikistan's remoteness, are the main obstacles to more robust economic relations. Turkey's main imports from Tajikistan are aluminum and cotton; sudden changes in world commodity prices therefore affect Tajikistan's production capacity, which in turn has a bearing on the volume of Turkish imports too. According to Tajik data, Turkey ranks fifth among Tajikistan's trade partners.

RUSSIA

Post–Cold War Turkish-Russian relations developed steadily in spite of differences of opinion and approaches on some important regional and international issues. Turkey and Russia started to develop bilateral relations through economic cooperation in the 1990s, creating a strong background for further progress in the political realm in the 2000s. The formation of a High Level Strategic Cooperation Council in 2010 and reciprocal lifting of visa requirements caused a rapid development of person-to-person contacts; approximately 4.5 million Russians visited Turkey in 2014. This cooperation has more recently been thrown into question by the downing of a Russian Su-24 fighter-bomber that had crossed into Turkish airspace on November 24, 2015, an event that sparked the biggest crisis in Russo-Turkish relations since the Cold War.

"The Joint Action Plan for Cooperation in Eurasia" signed between Turkey and Russia in 2001 is the most significant document to enhance bilateral coordination and cooperation in the region. This document allowed the two countries to extend their relations, their political consultations, and their experience in the field of economic cooperation into the Eurasian space. Enhanced dialogue and cooperation in Eurasia, they believed, would positively contribute to bring about peaceful, just, and lasting solutions to the problems in the region and help develop bilateral and multilateral economic relations between Ankara and Moscow.

Russia is Turkey's second largest individual trade partner after Germany, while Turkey ranks sixth in Russia's foreign trade. In 2014, the volume of trade between the two countries reached $31.2 billion. Turkey exports foodstuffs, textiles, and chemical products to Russia, while Turkish imports from Russia are generally oil, natural gas, petroleum products, steel, and iron. Russia has invested around $10 billion in the Turkish market, and Turkish investments in the Russian economy are of an approximately equal amount. Turkish contractors have already carried out some 1,576 projects in Russia with a total value of $56.4 billion.

The main area of cooperation between the two countries is in the field of energy. Around 65 percent of Turkey's energy imports are comprised of Russian oil and gas. Russia also started to construct the first nuclear power plant in Turkey in Akkuyu/Mersin. After the downing of the Russian Su-24 in late November 2015, there is some confusion about the status of this project. Russia has said that the construction was halted, which the Turkish side denied.

Enhanced relations between Turkey and Russia before late 2015 raised the question of Turkey's further integration with Russian-led projects in the region. To enhance its place and role in Eurasia, Turkey has always looked positively at Eurasian initiatives such as the Eurasian Economic Union (EEU), with a view to complementing its western vector with an enhanced eastern vision. Turkey has applied to become a Dialogue Partner of the SCO, though its interest in the EEU has not been less keen. Both Russian president Vladimir Putin and Kazakh president Nursultan Nazarbayev have mentioned a desire to see Turkey develop its relations with the Eurasian Economic Union.[25] Ankara has been cautious, however, with several officials pointing out that Turkey's membership in NATO as well as its aspiration to become a member of the European Union makes a rapprochement with the EEU more difficult to imagine.[26] Moreover, Ankara has not spelled out any interest in the EEU at the official level. Some Turkish scholars also worry that the EEU could prefigure efforts to restore Russian hegemony across the former Soviet Union.[27]

Low oil and gas prices, as well as international sanctions imposed over its intervention in Ukraine, have negatively impacted Russia's economy and, with it, Russo-Turkish trade relations. As Russian

25. İlknur Menlik, "Avrasya Birliği'ne doğru Türkiye," *Sabah*, May 26, 2014, http://www.sabah.com.tr/ekonomi/2014/05/26/avrasya-birligine-dogru-turkiye.

26. Ümit Nazmi Hazır, "Türkiye'nin Avrasya Ekonomik Birliği'ne üyeliği mümkün mü?," *Akademik Perspektif*, May 7, 2015, http://akademikperspektif.com/2015/05/07/turkiyenin-avrasya-ekonomik-birligine-uyeligi-mumkun-mu-2/.

27. Göktürk Tüysüzoğlu, "Bölgesel bir hegemonya girişimi: Avrasya Ekonomik Birliği," *Al Jazeera*, July 12, 2014, http://www.aljazeera.com.tr/gorus/bolgesel-bir-hegemonya-girisimi-avrasya-ekonomik-birligi.

purchasing power began to decline, Turkish exports to Russia contracted by 15 percent in 2014, with the overall decline reaching 34.6 percent by June 2015.[28]

Although Turkey and Russia have developed regular political consultations on issues affecting their shared Eurasian neighborhood, there are a variety of differences, ranging from Ukraine to Syria. In Syria, Turkey sees the regime of Bashar al-Assad as the main source of instability in the country and has opposed his inclusion in any transitional process.[29] Russia, on the other hand, has made it very clear that the Assad regime is the legitimate, elected representative of the Syrian people and that the Syrian army is an effective bulwark against the spread of the Islamic State. In an interview he gave to the Al Jazeera TV channel, President Erdoğan of Turkey questioned the justification of Russia's presence in Syria.[30]

Turkey also differs from Russia on the Ukrainian question, though Ankara has made efforts to limit the fallout of these disagreements. Turkey does not recognize the annexation of Crimea and is primarily concerned about the future of ethnically Turkic Crimean Tatars.

During his visit to Kiev on March 20, 2015, President Erdoğan reiterated the Turkish stance on the Crimean issue: "We have expressed our support for the territorial integrity, political union, and sovereignty of Ukraine, including Crimea, in every platform. We also wish for the continuation of Ukraine's stance of protecting the rights of all ethnic and religious minorities, especially Crimean Tatar Turks, who have proved their loyalty to their country during this crisis." Turkey offered Ukraine a loan of $50 million and an additional $10 million in humanitarian assistance.[31]

Energy relations have also been affected by political strains over Ukraine and Syria, with the Turkish Stream project being slowed.[32] Concerns about the overall tenor of Turkish-Russian relations were aggravated when Russian military aircraft violated Turkish airspace at the beginning of October 2015 during their air campaign in Syria,[33] culminating in the downing of the Russian Su-24 by the Turkish air force on November 24 of that year.

This incident has become a major setback to Turkish-Russian relations and will have consequences not only in the bilateral context but probably on the competition between Turkey and Russia in the Eurasian space in general.

---

28. Mehmet Çetingüleç, "Turkish exports plunge," *Al Monitor*, July 16, 2015, http://www.al-monitor.com/pulse/originals/2015/07/turkish-exports-plunge-despite-cheaper-currency.html#.

29. "No Turkey-Russia agreement on Syria," *Hürriyet Daily News*, September 19–20, 2015.

30. Erdoğan Şenel, "Rusya'nın sınırı olmayan Suriye'de ne işi var?," *Radikal*, October 4, 2015, http://blog.radikal.com.tr/dunya/rusyanin-siniri-olmayan-suriyede-ne-isi-var-113800.

31. "Turkey offers U.S. dollars 50 million loan to Ukraine, urges protection of Crimean Tatars," *Today's Zaman*, March 20, 2015, http://www.todayszaman.com/anasayfa_turkey-offers-50-mln-loan-to-ukraine-urges-protection-of-crimean-tatars_375784.html.

32. "Turkey, Russia 'freeze new gas pipeline talks,'" *Hürriyet Daily News*, September 12–13, 2015.

33. Ünal Çeviköz, "Testing times in Turkey's relations with Russia," *Turkish Policy Quarterly*, October 13, 2015, http://turkishpolicy.com/blog/7/testing-times-in-turkeys-relations-with-russia.

At the bilateral level, Moscow has made clear that it expects a formal apology, punishment, and compensation,[34] while Putin signed a decree imposing a range of sanctions on Turkish products and organizations.[35, 36] Moscow also suspended its visa-free agreement with Ankara over the incident and canceled a planned Putin-Erdoğan meeting in December 2015.

Russia has always been Turkey's main competitor in the Eurasian space. Recent deterioration in Russo-Turkish bilateral relations is bound to have repercussions in the post-Soviet sphere as well. The states of the Caucasus and Central Asia have always subordinated their bilateral relations with Turkey to the overall state of affairs between Russia and Turkey. As some of these states—namely, Kazakhstan and Kyrgyzstan (as well as Armenia)—are members of the Eurasian Economic Union, Moscow's sanctions on Turkey may create an indirect impact on their bilateral relations with Turkey too, further reducing Turkey's influence in Eurasia.

IRAN

Iran is another competitor for Turkey in the Eurasian geography. In the post–Cold War period, some of the Central Asian countries were looking not only to Turkey as a model, but to some degree to Iran as well.

Iran's international isolation over its nuclear program prevented Tehran from becoming a significant partner for the new Eurasian states. Nevertheless, Iran's presence in many regional organizations, including the ECO and SCO, as well as its slow but steady development of bilateral relations with many countries in the region give Tehran some leverage.

Although the current transport, communications, and energy infrastructure projects do not include Iran, they do not explicitly exclude it, either. The country's rich oil and gas resources may easily become a major source of increased interest and foreign investment, particularly after the recent agreement between Tehran and the P5+1 over the Iranian nuclear program and the anticipated end of international sanctions. The Turkish business community has already expressed interest in Iran, and Turkey will probably look for opportunities in the Iranian market, mainly in the development of its energy sector. As sanctions are lifted, Iran's South Pars energy field may open for foreign investment, creating new opportunities for Turkish companies.

Turkey and Iran have, so far, skillfully managed to separate their bilateral relations from their regional interests. Syria, however, appears to have become a source of tension, since the two countries have significant differences on the future of Syria.

---

34. In an interview given to Turkish daily *Cumhuriyet*, Andrei Karlov, the Russian ambassador in Ankara, explained the Russian position. He also claimed that the Russian pilot was killed by a Turk as he was coming down by parachute after being ejected from the shot plane. See "Rusya'nın 3 şartı var," *Cumhuriyet*, December 13, 2015, http://www.cumhuriyet.com.tr/haber/dunya/447673/Rusya_nin_3_sarti_var.html.

35. "Putin Türkiye'ye yaptırımları onayladı," *Avrupa Forum*, November 30, 2015, http://avrupaforum.org/putin-turkiyeye-yaptirimlari-onayladi/.

36. Paul Sonne and Emre Peker, "Russia's Vladimir Putin Places Sanctions Against Ankara Over Downing of Fighter Plane," *The Wall Street Journal*, November 29, 2015, http://www.wsj.com/articles/russian-president-vladimir-putin-calls-for-sanctions-against-turkey-1448736083.

CHINA

In recent years, China has assumed an important role in the economies of the Central Asian countries. Its emphasis on expanding transit through the Silk Road Economic Belt also extends to the South Caucasus and beyond through its interest in the Baku-Tbilisi-Kars railroad project. Chinese interest in Central Asia and its involvement in energy and transport projects extending through the Caucasus region indicate how China will be involved in developing its relations with the countries of the region in the future.

Most of the Central Asian countries look at China's Silk Road Economic Belt project favorably. They view China as a significant partner, particularly in the areas of know-how and technology transfer, as well as financing of transport and communication projects. China also looks to the Central Asian countries to reach out to the Caspian and the Middle East with a view to improving its access to energy supplies.

03

Turkey in a Reconnecting Eurasia

There are a number of projects that play a significant role in Turkey's integration with Eurasia through development of much-needed infrastructure in the fields of transport, transit, and communications.

MULTILATERAL COOPERATION

Among the welter of regional multilateral organizations in Eurasia, Turkey has pursued cooperation in particular with the Conference on Interaction and Confidence-Building Measures in Asia (CICA) and the SCO.

CONFERENCE ON INTERACTION AND CONFIDENCE-BUILDING MEASURES IN ASIA

Inspired by the OSCE in Europe, in October 1992 President Nursultan Nazarbayev of Kazakhstan invited the countries of Asia to join together with a view to developing mechanisms for security and cooperation. The initiative eventually led to the establishment of CICA (beginning with the convening of a working group in March 1995). In 1999, the 15 participating states adopted a "Declaration on Principles Guiding Relations between CICA Member States" and agreed to develop this initiative into a regional multilateral forum. In June 2002, 16 founding states convened at a summit meeting and signed the Almaty Act as the charter of CICA. Today, the organization has 26 member states and eight observer states.[1]

1. Member states of CICA are Afghanistan, Azerbaijan, Bahrain, Bangladesh, Cambodia, China, Egypt, India, Iran, Iraq, Israel, Jordan, Kazakhstan, Kyrgyzstan, Mongolia, Pakistan, Palestine, Qatar, Republic of Korea, Russia, Tajikistan, Thailand, Turkey, United Arab Emirates, Uzbekistan, and Vietnam. Observer states are Belarus, Indonesia, Japan, Malaysia, Philippines, Sri Lanka, Ukraine, and the United States. Observer organizations are the United Nations, OSCE, the League of Arab States, and the Parliamentary Assembly of the Turkic-Speaking Countries (TURKPA).

As a founding member of CICA, Turkey uses the organization to promote confidence-building measures in the areas of political-military cooperation, economic cooperation, environmental issues, humanitarian issues, terrorism, and human trafficking.

In 2010, President Nazarbayev requested that Turkey assume the chairmanship of CICA. Ankara took over the chairmanship from Kazakhstan at the Third Summit of the Conference on Interaction and Confidence-Building Measures in Asia, which was held in Istanbul on June 7–9, 2010.

During its chairmanship, Turkey sought to transform CICA into a much strengthened cooperation mechanism and an international structure that generates stability and a confidence-building atmosphere.[2] Although CICA is still far from matching the competencies of the OSCE in the Euro-Atlantic space, Turkey wishes to expand CICA's role by building on the experience of similar subregional cooperative structures, such as the Association of Southeast Asian Nations (ASEAN).

SHANGHAI COOPERATION ORGANIZATION

Established on June 15, 2001, the SCO currently has six members (China, Russia, Kyrgyzstan, Tajikistan, Kazakhstan, Uzbekistan), five observers (Afghanistan, Mongolia, Iran, India, Pakistan), and three dialogue partners (Turkey, Sri Lanka, and Belarus). Member states cover a geographical area of 60 percent of Eurasia, and their population comprises 25 percent of the world's total. Together with observers and dialogue partners, the SCO represents half of the world population. Member states' GDP amounts to 14.9 percent of global production.

Turkey applied for dialogue partner status in the SCO on May 11, 2012, and the SCO heads of state unanimously approved Ankara's request at the summit in Beijing on June 7, 2012. The agreement confirming Turkey's status envisages cooperation on areas such as regional security, combating terrorism and organized crime, prevention of drug trafficking, and economic and cultural cooperation.

During his tenure as prime minister, Erdoğan frequently referred to the SCO as the "new direction of Turkey." His rhetoric was in part a reaction against continued delays facing Turkey's accession to the European Union. As the center of global economic activity shifts further east, to Asia and the Pacific, Turkish officials also believe a more formalized relationship with the SCO may open new opportunities while reflecting the ambitions to pursue a "multifaceted foreign policy."

Turkey is the first and thus far only NATO member to develop an institutional relationship with the SCO. For the time being, Turkey does not anticipate seeking observer status or full membership. Turkish foreign ministry spokesman Levent Gümrükçü, in an answer to a question by the press on February 5, 2013, said:

> Turkey's relation with SCO is not an alternative to its relations with the EU or NATO and likewise, our existing relationships with these organizations are not

2. *Conference on Interaction and Confidence-Building Measures in Asia, Turkish Chairmanship: Constructing Cooperative Security in Asia,* http://www.cicaistanbul.org/default.en.mfa.

an obstacle to cooperation with SCO. Indeed, the EU has decided to develop relations with SCO in 2012, and this decision was emphasized in the mandate of the Special Representative for Central Asia. In his response to a question in this context, Anders Fogh Rasmussen, Secretary General of NATO, stated that there are no contradictions in this regard at all.[3]

INFRASTRUCTURE PROJECTS

Increasing trade relations between Europe and Asia has imparted new momentum to the construction of infrastructure projects connecting Central Asia, the Caspian basin, and the Black Sea. The EU-sponsored TRACECA is one of these initiatives along the east–west corridor. Starting from Bulgaria, Romania, and Ukraine, the TRACECA corridor encompasses Turkey as well and aspires to develop economic relations, trade, and transport communications by facilitating access to markets, ensuring traffic safety, and harmonizing transportation policies.[4] Through the Black Sea, the corridor reaches the ports of Poti and Batumi in Georgia, then connects to Turkey via the South Caucasus transport networks.

The TRACECA corridors encompass both the Baku-Tbilisi-Batumi and Baku-Tbilisi-Poti routes as well. These two railroads are further connected to European networks via Black Sea rail ferry lines linking Azerbaijan and Georgia to the west. Baku, meanwhile, will be connected by ferry to the ports of Aktau in Kazakhstan and Turkmenbashi in Turkmenistan on the eastern coast of the Caspian Sea under the TRACECA framework. The transportation networks of these countries end up in Uzbekistan, Kyrgyzstan, and Tajikistan, arriving at the borders of China and Afghanistan.

A further connection between Turkey and Georgia is being developed with the construction of the Baku-Tbilisi-Kars (BTK) railway project, which is expected to become operational in 2016. In its initial phase, this railroad is projected to carry 1 million passengers and 6.5 million tons of goods per year. By 2034 its capacity is estimated to reach 3 million passengers and 17 million tons of goods per year. BTK is intended to constitute an integral part of the "Iron Silk Road" of the twenty-first century. The aim is to enable producers in East Asia to access European markets through the Kazakhstan-China-Mongolia railway. Efforts to integrate the project with China's Silk Road Economic Belt are also under way.

A related project called *Lapis Lazuli* is planned to connect Afghanistan-Turkmenistan-Caspian Sea-Azerbaijan-Georgia, continuing either through ports on the Black Sea coast or through the BTK railroad to reach Europe.

---

3. Republic of Turkey, Ministry of Foreign Affairs, *QA-3, 5 February 2013, Statement of the Spokesman of the Ministry of Foreign Affairs of Turkey in Response to a Question Regarding Turkey's Dialogue Partnership to the Shanghai Cooperation Organization*, http://www.mfa.gov.tr/qa_3_-5-february-2013_-statement-of-the-spokesman-of-the -ministry-of-foreign-affairs-of-turkey-in-response-to-a-question-regarding-turkey_s-dialogue-partnership-to-the -shanghai-cooperation-organization.en.mfa.

4. TRACECA member states are Azerbaijan, Armenia, Georgia, Bulgaria, Kazakhstan, Kyrgyzstan, Moldova, Romania, Turkmenistan, Tajikistan, Turkey, Ukraine, Uzbekistan, and Mongolia.

BTK is not a part of TRACECA, however, since it excludes Armenia, and Armenian organizations in the United States successfully lobbied Congress to prevent U.S. financial institutions from funding the project.[5] Azerbaijan, Georgia, and Turkey consequently had to take on the burden of funding the BTK project themselves. As part of their cooperation related to BTK, in early 2015, the presidents of the three countries signed the Tbilisi Declaration, envisaging a regional cooperation process and mutual support on transportation, electric power, and natural gas to provide a long-term economic foundation for BTK.[6] The BTK project is also included in the Master Plan on the Trans-European Railway (TER) network sponsored by the United Nations Economic Commission for Europe (UNECE).

Turkey sees Kazakhstan as a potential partner in the transportation projects between Central Asia and the Caucasus. Ankara has approached Astana about linking up its rail network to the BTK railroad, which would create a rail corridor to East Asia through Kazakhstan. Kazakhstan also sees Turkey as a potential partner in its outreach to the west and has invited Turkey to participate in the Agreement on the "Development of Trans-Caspian International Transport Route (TITR) Coordination Committee," which was signed in November 2014. This corridor will connect Kazakhstan, Azerbaijan, Georgia, and Turkey from the terminals in the port of Aktau, through Azerbaijan and Akhalkalaki (Georgia) to Kars (Turkey), with further integration with the Marmaray project in Turkey under the Marmara Sea, creating a new trans-Caspian route linking the markets of Asia and Europe through Kazakhstan, the South Caucasus, and Turkey. Kazakhstan regards the accession of the Turkish railways to the Coordination Committee as a step forward in promoting and improving multimodal transportation, containerization, removal of barriers, and access to international markets.[7]

ENERGY

Although Turkey is not a significant energy producer, its geographical location at the crossroads of east-west and north-south energy corridors gives it an opportunity to become a crucial energy hub for Eurasia as a whole. Turkey is a net energy importer, and among OECD member countries, Turkey's energy demand has been the fastest growing in the last 10 years, with energy demand projected to double in the next decade. Today, around 26 percent of Turkey's total energy demand is met by domestic resources, while the rest is provided from a diversified portfolio of imports.[8] The TANAP project is the backbone of European Union's Southern Gas Corridor (SGC). Designed to reduce EU dependence on Russian gas, TANAP also plays a prominent role in Turkey's policy of

5. "South Caucasus Integration and Open Railroads Act of 2005," June 20, 2005, U.S. Library of Congress, https://www.govtrack.us/congress/bills/109/hr3361.

6. Georgian Ministry of Foreign Affairs, *The Tbilisi Declaration on Common Vision for Regional Cooperation*, (Tbilisi, Georgia, February 7, 2007), http://www.civil.ge/eng/article.php?id=14588.

7. Press Office of JSC "NC" "KTZ" (Kazakh Railways), *The meeting on the development of the Trans-Caspian international transport route*, October 21, 2014, www.railways.kz/en/node/7771.

8. Republic of Turkey, Ministry of Foreign Affairs, *Turkey's Energy Strategy*, last updated 2011, http://www.mfa.gov.tr/turkeys-energy-strategy.en.mfa.

seeking to become an energy hub. TANAP not only ensures the transfer of gas from the Caspian region, but could also be expanded through connection to additional resources in the Middle East. One such potential contributor is the Kurdistan Regional Government in northern Iraq. Over the longer term, Iran could also become a contributor, once sanctions on its exports are removed and Tehran can attract new investment. This aspect of TANAP enhances the diversification of routes and supplies, hence enhancing the energy security of Europe.

The first natural gas through the TANAP pipeline is expected to arrive in Turkey in 2018 and then further on to Europe in 2020. The pipeline will initially carry 16 billion cubic meters (bcm) of gas per year, extracted from phase II production from Azerbaijan's Shah Deniz field, of which 6 bcm will be for Turkish domestic consumption and the remaining 10 bcm will be exported to European markets. The total pipeline capacity will increase to 23 bcm in 2023 and 31 bcm in 2026.

Turkey also seeks to eventually feed Turkmen gas into TANAP. At a meeting in Ashgabat in May 2015, the Turkish, Azerbaijani, and Turkmen energy ministers, together with the deputy EU Commissioner for Energy Union, agreed to form a working group to facilitate the preparation of a framework agreement for Turkmenistan's participation in the project. The first meeting of this working group took place in Brussels in July 2015, with the participation of Georgia as well.

In 2009, Turkey and Russia agreed in principle to develop the South Stream pipeline, to be constructed under the Black Sea through Bulgaria, to supply Europe with up to 64 bcm of natural gas per year. Though Turkey was also participating in the European Union's Southern Gas Corridor, it saw South Stream as a boon that would allow it to access additional sources of gas while enhancing transit competition and furthering Turkey's energy hub aspirations. South Stream also bypassed Ukraine, which would potentially be completely cut off from Russian gas transit, and would not introduce any new suppliers other than Russia. These features, combined with Gazprom's ownership of both the pipeline and the gas supplied through it, led the European Commission and many European states to oppose building South Stream. However, Turkey gave permission for the launching of feasibility studies for passing South Stream through its territorial waters in the Black Sea in December 2011.[9]

In the face of ongoing EU opposition, Gazprom announced in December 2014 that it was canceling South Stream and replacing it with a new pipeline project dubbed Turkish Stream, which would be constructed across the Black Sea and then via Turkey to the Greek border. Some Turkish officials believed that the new project could help Turkey to realize its ambitions to become a regional energy hub, though the Turkish Foreign Ministry was more prudent, approving the project in principle but voicing concern that it could undermine Turkey's objective of attracting Iraqi, Iranian, Turkmen, and Azeri natural gas.[10] This hesitation delayed the signing of any official document between Russia and Turkey, and finally Russia had to postpone the agreement. Although Russia

9. Onur Çobanlı, "Turkey in the Eurasian Energy Game," *Global Relations Forum: Young Academics Program Policy Papers*, series no. 1 (November 2014), http://www.gif.org.tr/Documents/Turkey%20in%20the%20Eurasian%20Energy%20Game.pdf.

10. Serkan Demirtaş, "Turkish Stream postponed because of Russia, not Turkey," *Hürriyet Daily News*, September 16, 2015, http://www.hurriyetdailynews.com/turkish-stream-postponed-because-of-russia-not-turkey.aspx?PageID=238&NID=88523&NewsCatID=429.

blamed the political crisis in Turkey after the June 7, 2015 elections for the delay, it appears that Ankara has been having cold feet due to concern about Turkish Stream's possible negative effects on future projects.[11] After the shooting down of the Russian fighter jet by Turkey, the project is now entirely suspended.

---

11. Ibid.

04

Conclusion

Turkey has been one of the main contenders for influence in Eurasia in the post–Cold War era. In spite of its limited resources, Turkey has been quite adept in advancing the economic development and integration of the post-Soviet countries into the world system. Turkey's policy in Eurasia in the last 25 years has had its ups and downs, but Ankara has carried on. In the initial phase, Turkey was quite excited to have discovered a new Turkic "hinterland" with historic, cultural, and linguistic affinities. In time, however, the emergence of Islamist tendencies in Turkey's domestic politics under the AKP contradicted the post-Soviet countries' secular political traditions. Russia also started to revert to a more assertive foreign policy in the region, leaving Turkey and other regional powers fewer opportunities.

Turkey has launched many multilateral initiatives that have helped the Eurasian states develop cooperation schemes based on regional and subregional mechanisms. The Black Sea Economic Cooperation organization and the Turkic Council are examples of such initiatives. In time, the experience of Eurasian countries in working together under the auspices of such multilateral structures helped encourage them to look for further integration opportunities, opening the way for the development of several new infrastructure projects. Turkey, due to its geography at the crossroads of continents between the East and the West, will inevitably be at the epicenter of many of these projects in the fields of transport, communications, and energy.

Today Eurasia retains its importance in Turkey's foreign policy objectives. Turkey's Eurasian vision, however, faces two principal challenges. On the one hand, Russia, China, and, to a lesser degree, Iran will continue to be significant actors in the region. Other global actors such as the United States and the European Union will not remain indifferent to Eurasian politics, either. Turkey's success, therefore, will depend in part on its ability to harmonize its approach with those of other actors in the region. Turkey will additionally have to develop its policies in Eurasia prudently and in tandem with its main strategic objective—namely, to become a member of the European Union. Turkey and the European Union, united in the formulation of their policies in Eurasia, will perform more successfully.

In addition, developments in the Middle East have created more acute problems for the international community in general and Turkey in particular. The upheaval across the Arab world has failed to establish democratic rule and has instead sparked extremism, conflict, and the flow of millions of refugees out of the region, many of them into Turkey. Five years ago, the Arab Middle East contained many authoritarian regimes. Today it contains many failed states. Syria and Iraq, facing the growing threat of the Islamic State's terror, share a long common border with Turkey in the south and have sent between them upward of two million refugees across the border into Turkey. The upheaval in the region is also breathing new life into Ankara's conflict with the Kurds. In the short to medium term, therefore, the Middle Eastern crisis will continue to be at the center of Turkey's foreign policy. This may result in the further allocation of human and financial resources to the region. Eventually, this reallocation is likely to result in a diminution of Turkey's influence in Eurasia. Turkey under the circumstances will probably remain content to focus on the development of infrastructure projects in its vicinity, mainly centered on transport and energy, in order to reassure its future role as a viable partner both for the East and the West.

About the Author

Ünal Çeviköz is a former Turkish diplomat who retired from government service in September 2014. He began his career as second secretary at the Turkish embassy in Moscow in 1981. He served as the chief of section at the East European Department of the Turkish Ministry of Foreign Affairs (MFA) and later as counselor of the Turkish embassy in Sofia, Bulgaria. In 1989, he was detached from the MFA to work in NATO's International Secretariat, first at the Economics Directorate and then the Political Directorate as an East European expert. In 1994, he was commissioned with launching the NATO Information Office in Moscow, after which he prepared the NATO-Russia Founding Act. On return to the MFA in 1997, he worked as the head of the Balkan Department and then as the deputy director general for Caucasus and Central Asia. He has served as the Turkish ambassador to Azerbaijan (2001–2004), to Iraq (2004–2006), and to the United Kingdom (2010–2014). He was also the deputy undersecretary for bilateral political affairs at the Turkish MFA from 2007 to 2010 and prepared the protocols signed between Turkey and Armenia. Currently he is president of Ankara Policy Centre.

www.ingramcontent.com/pod-product-compliance
Lightning Source LLC
Chambersburg PA
CBHW081437270326
41932CB00019B/3244